MW01130275

leila

A Tuareg Child

By Hervé Giraud
Photos by Jean-Charles Rey

BLACKBIRCH PRESS
A part of Gale, Cengage Learning

 GALE
CENGAGE Learning

Detroit • New York • San Francisco • New Haven, Conn • Waterville, Maine • London

For more information, contact
Blackbirch Press
27500 Drake Rd.
Farmington Hills, MI 48331-3535
Or you can visit our Internet site at gale.cengage.com

Every effort has been made to trace the owners of copyrighted material.

Photo Credits: All photos © Jean-Charles Rey except page 6, Corel Corporation; Table of Contents collage: EXPLORER/Boutin (upper left); François Goalec (upper middle and right); Muriel Nicolotti (bottom left); CIRIC/Michel Gauvry (bottom middle); CIRIC/Pascal Deloche (bottom right)

LIBRARY OF CONGRESS CATALOGING-IN-PUBLICATION DATA

Giraud, Hervé.
  Leila : a Tuareg child / by Hervé Giraud.
    p. cm. — (Children of the world)
  ISBN 1-4103-0545-7 (hardcover : alk. paper)
  1. Children, Tuareg—Juvenile literature. 2. Tuaregs—Social life and customs—Juvenile literature. I. Title. II. Series: Children of the world (Blackbirch Press)

  DT346.T7G57 2005
  966'.004933—dc22

                                                    2005000702

Printed in the United States of America
2 3 4 5 6 7 12 11 10 09 08

Contents

ARCTIC

OCEAN

ICELAND

SWEDEN

NORWAY

FINLAND

DENMARK

ESTONIA

LATVIA

LITHUANIA

IRELAND U.K. NETH. GERMANY POLAND BELARUS

BELGIUM LUX. CZECH

SWITZ. AUSTRIA SLOVAKIA UKRAINE

FRANCE SLOVENIA HUNGARY MOLDOVA

ITALY CROATIA ROMANIA

BOSNIA SERBIA BULGARIA

PORTUGAL SPAIN MONTENEGRO MACEDONIA

ALBANIA GREECE

RUSSIA

KAZAKHSTAN

MONGOLIA

NORTH KOREA

SOUTH KOREA

JAPAN

PACIFIC

GEORGIA

CYPRUS ARMENIA AZERBAIJAN

TURKEY

LEBANON SYRIA

UZBEKISTAN KYRGYZSTAN

TURKMENISTAN TAJIKISTAN

MOROCCO

TUNISIA

ISRAEL

IRAQ

JORDAN KUWAIT

IRAN

AFGHANISTAN

CHINA

TAIWAN

Canary Islands

ALGERIA

LIBYA EGYPT

SAUDI ARABIA

QATAR

U.A.E.

PAKISTAN

NEPAL BHUTAN

WESTERN SAHARA

OMAN

INDIA

MAURITANIA

MALI NIGER

YEMEN

BANGLADESH

MYANMAR LAOS

VIETNAM

SENEGAL

CHAD SUDAN

ERITREA

GAMBIA

BURKINA

DJIBOUTI

CAMBODIA

PHILIPPINES

GUINEA BISSAU GUINEA

BENIN NIGERIA

SOMALIA

ETHIOPIA

BRUNEI

MALAYSIA

SIERRA LEONE

IVORY COAST

TOGO

GHANA CAMEROON

CENTRAL AFRICAN REPUBLIC

UGANDA

SINGAPORE

LIBERIA

EQUATORIAL GUINEA

KENYA

INDONESIA

PAPUA NEW GUINEA

SAO TOME & PRINCIPE

GABON CONGO

RWANDA

ZAIRE BURUNDI

ATLANTIC

TANZANIA

ANGOLA ZAMBIA

FIJI

MADA

MALAWI

NAMIBIA

ZIMBABWE

BOTSWANA MOZAMBIQUE

NEW CALEDONIA

AUSTRALIA

SWAZILAND

SOUTH AFRICA

LESOTHO

OCEAN

NEW ZEALAND

Land of the Tuaregs

Rabat

MOROCCO

TUNISIA

Mediterranean Sea

ALGERIA

Tripoli

LIBYA

The Land of the Tuaregs

MALI

NIGER

Tombouctou

CHAD

Niamey

Bamako

BURKINA FASO

Ougadougou

NIGERIA

Facts About the Tuaregs

The Tuaregs: A nomadic Berber people organized into tribes. Nomadic herders, they lead their herds of animals through the Sahara and the semidesert zones of the Sahal.

Alphabet: Tifinagh
Language: Tamashek (the only Berber language with an alphabet)
Population: 2,000,000
Religion: Sunni Islam
Where they live: Algeria (Hoggar and Tassili), Libya, Niger, Burkina Faso,

The Sahara Desert, Land of the Tuaregs

The Sahara Desert may look uninhabited but it is the home of the Tuareg nomads.

The Sahara Desert may be bleak, but it can support life. In fact, Tuareg nomads live there. They sleep under heavy hide tents. They raise camels, donkeys, and goats. Because they are nomads, they move about constantly in search of water and pastures for their animals.

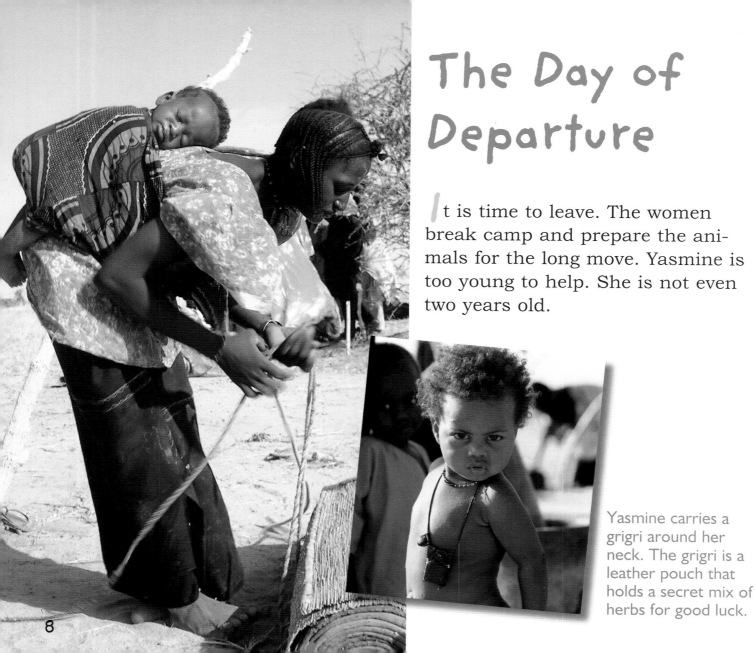

The Day of Departure

It is time to leave. The women break camp and prepare the animals for the long move. Yasmine is too young to help. She is not even two years old.

Yasmine carries a grigri around her neck. The grigri is a leather pouch that holds a secret mix of herbs for good luck.

Leila, her older sister, helps her mother attach a pack on a donkey. Then she covers the pack with blankets to make a comfortable seat for the journey.

Riding Camels

A camel rider has to mount the animal while it is lying down. When a camel is standing, the saddle is six and a half feet (two meters) above the ground. The camel rider pulls the reins to make the animal lie down. Once the rider is on the camel's back, he or she gives a sharp tug and shouts at the camel. The camel first straightens its back legs, then its front legs, and gets going with a slow rocking pace.

A camel has to lie down in order for its rider to mount.

To get off the camel, the rider must make it lie down again. The rider gives the camel a strong push with his foot on the back of its neck.

The women and children travel on the donkeys along with all the camping gear.

In order to get off the camel, the rider gives it a strong push on the neck to make it lie down again.

11

The Journey

The tribe has left for a long trip in extreme heat. It can be 122 degrees Fahrenheit (50 degrees Centigrade) in the shade!

People and animals move slowly across the sparse landscape.

Leila is traveling on a heavily loaded donkey.

Sometimes a Tuareg has to run to round up an animal that has strayed or gone too far ahead.

Some animals are hobbled with a rope around their legs so they will not run too fast. This is how Tuaregs get the young animals to peacefully follow the herd.

Putting Up the Tents

The tents are made of hide. The hides are stretched over stakes pushed into the sand. Once the rugs are rolled out, the beds put up, and

Right: As soon as they arrive, the Tuaregs must put up the tents.

Below: The tents are positioned in a north/south direction and open on the side away from the Sun.

the clothes hung up, the camp is finally finished. It is exhausting work because it is so hot. Everyone sits in the shade of the tents to rest and chat. The men discuss what chores need to be done the next day.

The women sit with the children.

Yasmine can take a nap.

Water in the Wells

One of the main jobs of the Tuaregs is to find water. The wells of the Sahara are as rare as they are deep.

The length of the ropes shows how deep they must go to reach water. The water is sometimes a couple of hundred feet (several dozen meters) underground.

The ropes are tied to the donkeys. The donkeys back away from the well and pull up the heavy leather water skins.

There is lots of activity around the well. People and animals gather around the well, happy to finally quench their thirst.

Water in the Rivers

In the desert, water is not found only in wells. In good years, seasonal rains fill the dry riverbeds, which become a good water source for people and animals.

The goats can finally drink. To graze, they need to leave the water hole.

When the water in the rivers is drink-able, it is the children's job to fill the guerbas, the large water skins.

Water seeps through the skin of the guerba. That evaporation keeps the water cool.

The Tuaregs know that water is some-times hidden a couple of inches (a few centimeters) under the sand. They dig a hole, and the water appears.

Below: Water is always scarce. After a long trek across the Sahara, a thirsty camel can drink as much as 42 gallons (160 liters) of water.

In the desert, a person must drink 1 gallon (3 liters) of water a day.

Tuareg Women

The constant activity around the wells is noisy. The Tuaregs camp away from them to avoid the noise.

Carrying water is a job everyone shares. Every day, Leila rides her donkey to the wells. She fills her guerba with water and then firmly ties it under the donkey's belly.

Yasmine watches the women prepare the meal. Leila slowly pounds the grains of millet with a mortar. It takes a long time.

After it is sifted, the dark flour will be used for pancakes.

Sometimes the women stretch a skin over their mortars. They then use them as drums to beat out ancestral rhythms.

Camp Life

Unlike other Muslims, Tuareg men wear a veil. Called a cheche, the veil is a piece of cloth that is 16 feet (5 meters) long. The men wrap the veil around the head.

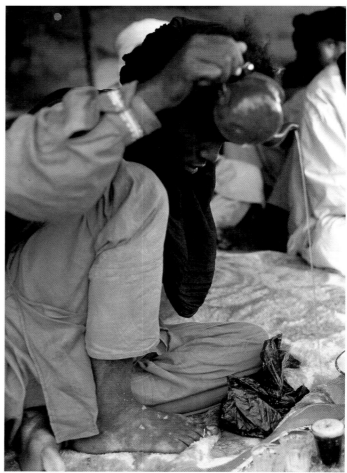

It protects them from the sun and blowing sand. They almost never take it off, not even when they are in the tent.

The Tuaregs make many of their daily tools. Yasmine's father carves wooden spoons with a tool that he made himself. He also weaves special cloths to cover the camels on festival days.

The children help out with camp life. They watch over the herds, milk the cows, and build fires.

This does not keep them from bathing in the rivers and having fun playing in the water. In many ways, they are just like children all over the world.

Other Books in the Series

Arafat: A Child of Tunisia

Asha: A Child of the Himalayas

Avinesh: A Child of the Ganges

Ballel: A Child of Senegal

Basha: A Hmong Child

Frederico: A Child of Brazil

Ituko: An Inuit Child

Kradji: A Child of Cambodia

Kuntai: A Masai Child

Madhi: A Child of Egypt

Thanassis: A Child of Greece

Tomasino: A Child of Peru